IQ Brainteasers

Are you ready to tackle a fiendish collection of word and number puzzles and stretch your brain powers to the limit?

Start at page one and work your way through the increasingly difficult brainteasers, increasing your skill levels as you progress. There are a full set of answers at the back of the book – but try not to take a sneaky peek!

Good luck!!

KoganPage

LONDON PHILADELPHIA NEW DELHI

Published in Great Britain in 2012 by Kogan Page Limited

Kogan Page Limited
120 Pentonville Road
London N1 9JN
United Kingdom
www.koganpage.com

© 2012, Arcturus Publishing Limited

ISBN
978 0 7494 6785 2

Typeset by Graphicraft Limited, Hong Kong
Printed and bound in India by Replika Press, Pvt Ltd

1. Odd One Out

Which number is the odd one out in each oval?

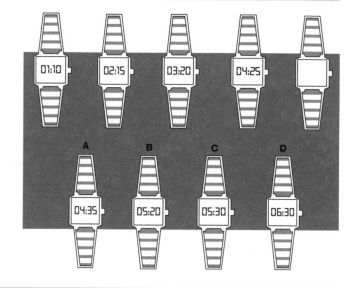

2. Watch Out

Look carefully at the sequence of watches and fill in the blank.

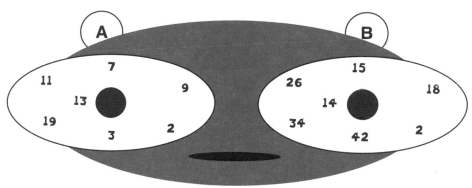

3. Pyramid Poser

Work out which number goes at the top of the third pyramid?

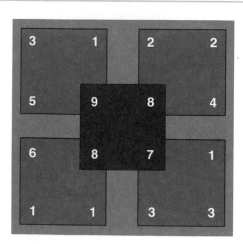

4. All Square

Here is a complete puzzle - work out why it contains these numbers. (Clue: The centre square holds the answer.)

5. Add-A-Letter

Add the same letter to all these words to make a brand new one. e.g. The letter 't' can be added to moral to make mortal.

SILL   HORN

SAND   TOO

RIM   FLUE

PLEA   RUE

6. Hidden Words

The name of a gemstone has been hidden in each of these sentences. Can you use your powers of observation and find them all?
e.g. A man's name has been hidden in this sentence: 'We hadn't given up hope terriers would be banned from the dog show next week.'

1 - Rub your eyes if you don't believe it

2 - Over christmas the wages are good. I am on double time.

3 - When you stop, always check in your mirror.

4 - From the cliff top, azure waters could be seen for miles.

5 - I can make a rabbit appear like magic.

7. Odd One Out

Which of these cities is the odd one out and why?

ROME   MELBOURNE   PARIS   LONDON   MADRID

8. First & Last

Which letter can replace the last letter of each word in the first column and the first letter of each word in the second column?
Write your answer in the box in the middle and make a new word going down.

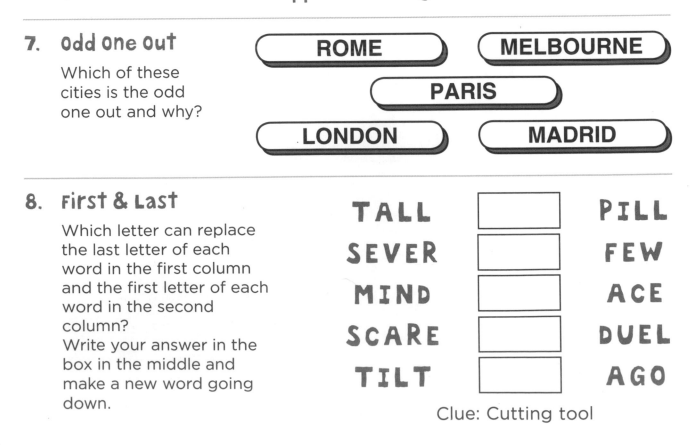

TALL		PILL
SEVER		FEW
MIND		ACE
SCARE		DUEL
TILT		AGO

Clue: Cutting tool

4

9. Dominoes

By counting the dots on these dominoes, can you work out which of the six spare pieces completes the sequence?

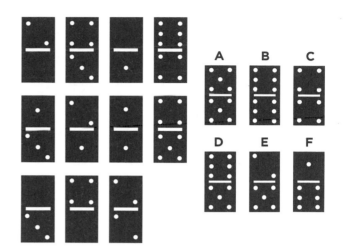

10. Cross Over

Which number is missing from each puzzle?

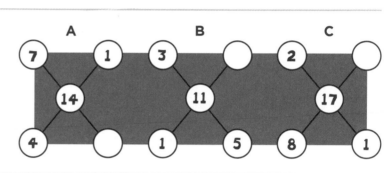

11. Tri-Pie

Which number is missing from the empty segment? (Clue: Look at the matching segments on each circle.)

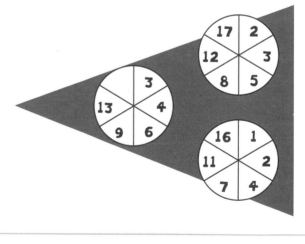

12. Number Box

Complete this number box by adding the correct number. (Clue: The puzzle works up and down as well as side to side!)

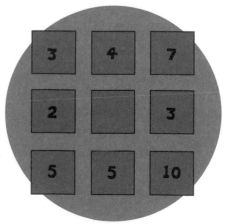

13. All Star

By using the first two stars as a guide, can you complete this puzzle?

3		2		45	10
21	6	6	4		
9	15	20	12	20	35

14. Circles

Which number is needed to finish the puzzle?

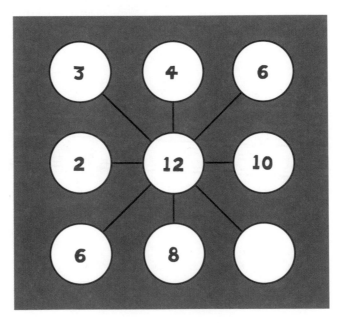

15. Boxing Clever

Which number completes this sequence?

2   3   5   9   ?

16. crossword

A regular crossword for you to enjoy. Try working it out by using the clues, but if you get stuck, the answers appear on the bottom of the page in alphabetical order.

Across

1 - Animal with scales and fins (4)
5 - Very hard wood (4)
8 - Gradually wear away (5)
10 - Our continent (6)
11 - Thin, pointed piece of ice hanging down (6)
12 - Soil in which plants grow (5)
14 - Container for pencils (4)
16 - Kiln for drying hops (4)
19 - Sloping platform (4)
20 - Diesel oil (4)
21 - Germany's neighbour (7)
22 - Better than any other (4)
24 - Kiss quickly (4)
26 - Line of coral just below the sea's surface (4)
28 - Swelling on the eyelid (4)
30 - A play in which most of the words are sung (5)
34 - Stop working due to old age (6)
35 - Deer's horn (6)
36 - Minister's house (5)
37 - Bigger amount (4)
38 - Knob on the sole of a football boot (4)

Down

1 - Give food to a person (4)
2 - A small river (6)
3 - Size of a flat surface (4)
4 - Get a book ready for printing (4)
6 - Words that explain why you have done something wrong (6)
7 - Was aware of (4)
8 - Sharp-pointed sword
9 - Sound that bounces off something solid (4)
13 - Style of jazz music (7)
14 - Pole tossed at Highland Games (5)
15 - Sudden outbreak (5)
17 - Change the use of something (5)
18 - Ceasefire (5)
23 - Slender game dog (6)
25 - Hole for threading laces through (6)
27 - Document with spaces to write in (4)
28 - Sensible (4)
29 - Percussion instrument (4)
31 - Fuel cut from bogs (4)
32 - Coarse file (4)
33 - Barney Rubble's friend, - - - Flintstone (4)

ADAPT
ANTLER
AREA
AUSTRIA
BEST
CABER
CASE
DERV
DRUM
EARTH
ECHO
EDIT
EPEE
ERODE

EUROPE
EXCUSE
EYELET
FEED
FISH
FORM
FRED
ICICLE
KNEW
MANSE
MORE
OAST
OPERA
PEAT

PECK
RAGTIME
RAMP
RASP
REEF
RETIRE
SANE
SETTER
SPATE
STREAM
STUD
STYE
TEAK
TRUCE

17. Five Star

We have taken a letter away from each star and replaced it with a question mark. Can you work out which letter is needed to complete the word in each shape?

(Clue: Look for things you might find in the garden)

18. Rogue Word

Work out which one of these words does not belong in this group.

QUICK

SPEEDY

FAST

CHARMER

RAPID

SWIFT

19. Anagram Timer

The answer to each of the clues is an anagram of the word above and below it, plus or minus one letter.

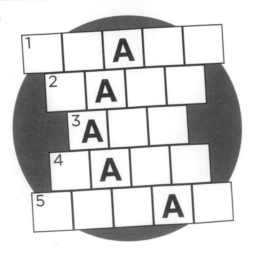

1 - To sweet talk

2 - Injure, damage

3 - Upper limb

4 - Female horse

5 - Vision seen in sleep

20. Missing Numbers

Which numbers are missing from the empty grid?
(Clue: Look at the matching segments – the middle circle is the link!)

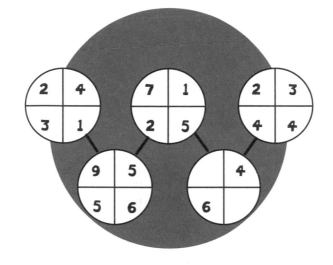

21. Honeycomb

Which number is the odd one out?

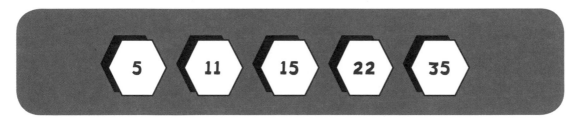

22. Hole Numbers

Complete this puzzle by adding the correct number to the empty circle.
(Clue: Straight thinking will not help you with this one!)

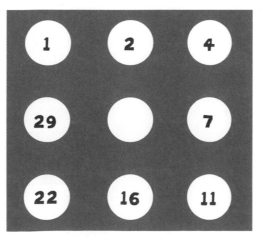

23. Proverbs

Here are three very famous proverbs with some missing words. From the choices we have given you can you complete them all?

A - - - is as good as a - - -".

Every - - - is allowed one - - -".

Great - - - from little acorns - - -".

| DOG | OAKS | MISS | BITE | GROW | MILE |

24. Opposites Attract

Match the four words on the left with a word of opposite meaning on the right.

OUT	LIGHT
DARK	SLOW
SWEET	IN
FAST	SOUR

25. Mix-Up

Unravel the letters to find four vegetables.

| TORACR | SEEDW |
| BAGACEB | RNPASIP |

26. Tri-Pie

Which number is missing from the empty segment? (Clue: Look at the matching segments on each circle.)

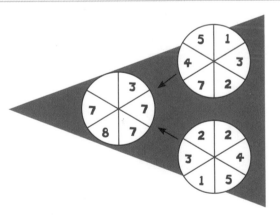

27. Number Box

Complete this number box by adding the correct number. (Clue: The puzzle works up and down as well as side to side!)

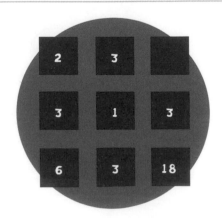

28. Add-A-Letter

Add the same letter to all these words to make a brand new one.
e.g. The letter 't' can be added to moral to make mortal.

CATER   SLAT
PAT   SPLIT
ICE   PIE
DUE   BET

29. Hidden Words

The name of a bird has been hidden in each of these sentences. Can you use your powers of observation and find them all?
e.g. A man's name has been hidden in this sentence: 'We hadn't given up hope terriers would be banned from the dog show next week.'

1 - Deciding to quit smoking, Joe took his final puff in March.
2 - After hearing Tom's plea, Glen let the matter drop.
3 - Sarah sat on the bench awkwardly.
4 - Andrew felt ashamed as he put back items he stole.
5 - As John scores par, rows erupt on the golf course.

30. Figure-It-Out

Which three-figure answer is missing from the empty box?

147	385	238
701	896	195
278	588	310
876		113

31. Shape Up

Find the missing number to complete the puzzle.

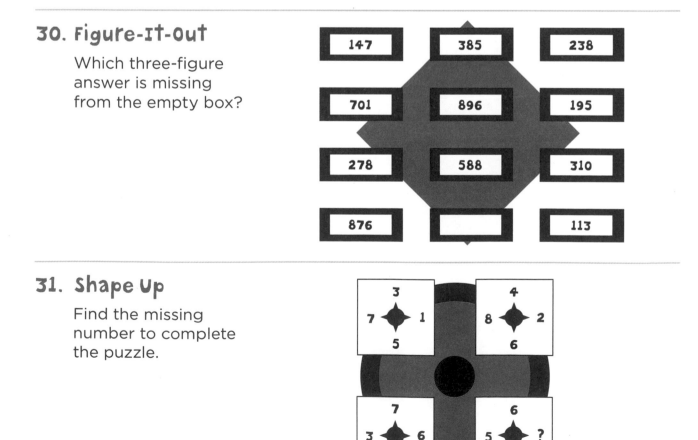

32. crossword

A regular crossword for you to enjoy. Try working it out by using the clues, but if you get stuck, the answers appear on the bottom of the page in alphabetical order.

Across

1 - Line of people one behind the other (4)
5 - Person in charge (4)
8 - Indicate (5)
10 - Clothes (6)
11 - Boil over with anger (6)
12 - Messenger sent by God (5)
14 - Actor, - - - Bean (4)
16 - Two things that belong together (4)
19 - British nobleman (4)
20 - Spot of ink spilt on something (4)
21 - Strong wind storm (7)
22 - Container for cut flowers (4)
24 - Cheerless, dingy (4)
26 - Novel's main character (4)
28 - University official (4)
30 - In which place? (5)
34 - TV star, - - - Turner (6)
35 - Heart disease (6)
36 - Quick, speedy (5)
37 - Move round (4)
38 - Used to be (4)

Down

1 - Flat open tart (4)
2 - More recent (6)
3 - Word said at the end of a prayer (4)
4 - Otherwise (4)
6 - Popular soup flavour (6)
7 - Appear (4)
8 - Gulf country, capital Tehran (4)
9 - Short sudden cry (4)
13 - Hard rock (7)
14 - Prince Andrew's ex-wife (5)
15 - Make different (5)
17 - Place to live in (5)
18 - Ancient Italian (5)
23 - Section (6)
25 - Deep steep-sided valley (6)
27 - Michael - - -, footballer (4)
28 - Declare to be false (4)
29 - Agreement, treaty (4)
31 - Soft covering that grows on the head (4)
32 - Speed of progress (4)
33 - Country road (4)

ABODE
ALTER
AMEN
ANGEL
ANGINA
ANTHEA
ATTIRE
BLOT
BOSS
DEAN
DENY
DRAB
EARL
ELSE

FILE
FLAN
GRANITE
HAIR
HERO
IMPLY
IRAN
LANE
LATTER
NIFTY
OWEN
OXTAIL
PACT
PAIR

RATE
RAVINE
ROMAN
SARAH
SEAN
SECTOR
SEEM
SEETHE
TORNADO
TURN
VASE
WERE
WHERE
YELP

33. Wheel Spin

Which letter replaces the question mark and completes the word?

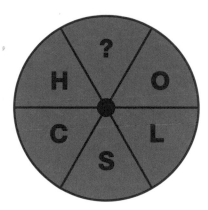

34. Take Away

What number goes in the middle oval?
(Clue: It has got nothing to do with sums!)

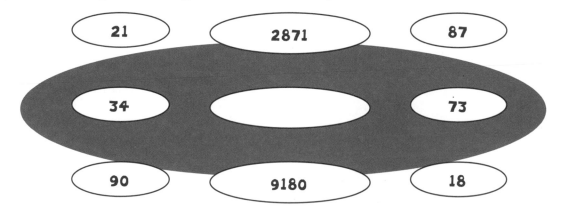

21	2871	87
34		73
90	9180	18

35. Dotty!

Which of the bottom numbers will go into the centre dot?
(Clue: Look at both sides of the grid.)

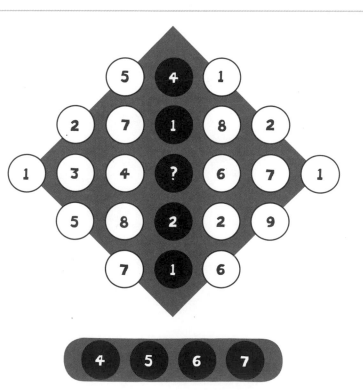

36. Vowel Play

All the vowels have been taken out of this crossword and placed in boxes next to the grid. Can you replace them all in their correct positions?

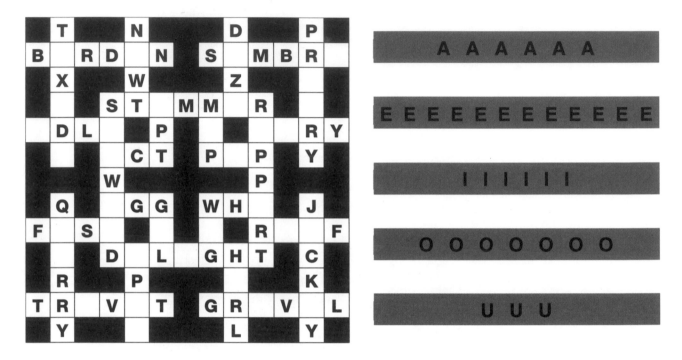

A A A A A A

E E E E E E E E E E E

I I I I I I

O O O O O O O

U U U

---

37. Next-In-Line

Which of the words below will logically follow on from these?

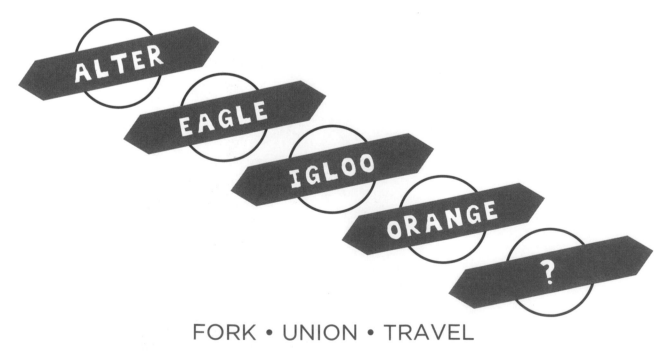

ALTER

EAGLE

IGLOO

ORANGE

?

FORK • UNION • TRAVEL

38. Line Up

Using the same rule for every row, can you fill in the empty octagons?

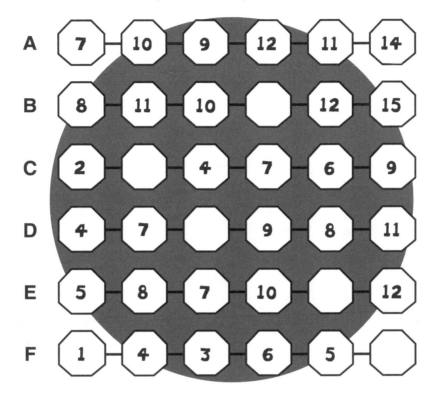

39. Change It

Replace the question mark with the correct number.
(Clue: Look at the relationship between the numbers in each segment.)

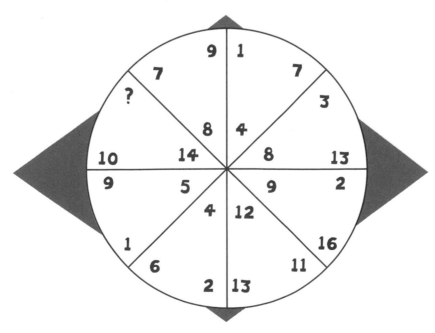

40. codebreaker

Every letter of the alphabet has been replaced with a number. Your job is to work out which number represents each letter and write it in the grid. We have entered the word NEAT so you know that 13 = N, 9 = E, 18 = A and 6 = T. If you get stuck there are two extra letters at the bottom of the page.

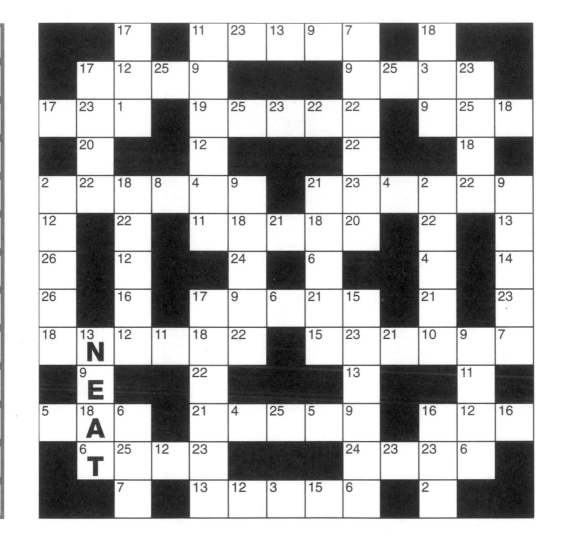

1	2	3	4	5	6	7	8	9	10	11	12	13
					T			E				N

14	15	16	17	18	19	20	21	22	23	24	25	26
				A								

25 = R 22 = L

41. Scrambled!

The answers to these clues have all been scrambled up.
Can you work out what each answer is?

1 **RIRGDEOP** Breakfast food

2 **OLREDHSU** Part of the body

3 **TACAPIL** Main town

4 **RHTYISO** Study of past events

5 **AFNUFRI** Amusement park

6 **GIACMAIN** Wizard

7 **KOETCP EOYMN** Child's allowance (6,5)

8 **ANUPYPH** Sad

9 **RIOTSUT** Holidaymaker

10 **BHGUERONI** Person next door

11 **TNEAENC** School cafe

12 **AINOTST** Police building

42. Options

Which of the three numbers at the bottom will complete this puzzle?
(Clue: Try looking up and down.)

43. Five Star

We have taken a letter away from each star and replaced it with a question mark. Can you work out which letter is needed to complete the word in each shape?
(Clue: Look for things that fly)

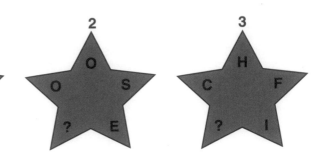

44. Rogue Word

Work out which one of these words does not belong in this group.

FRIGHT   HORROR   SCARE

TERROR   ALARM   WASTE

45. Rogue Number

In each square we have added a rogue number. Can you work out which one it is?

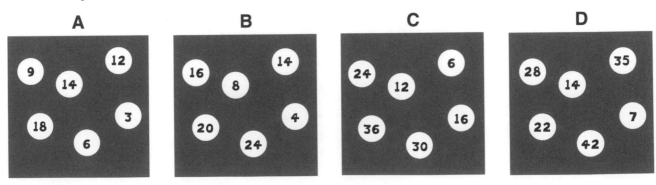

A
9 12 14 18 3 6

B
16 14 8 20 4 24

C
24 6 12 36 16 30

D
28 35 14 22 7 42

46. Missing Link

Which number completes this chain?

3   5   9   15   23   33   45   ?

47. Star Struck

Using the first two stars as an example, find the missing number.

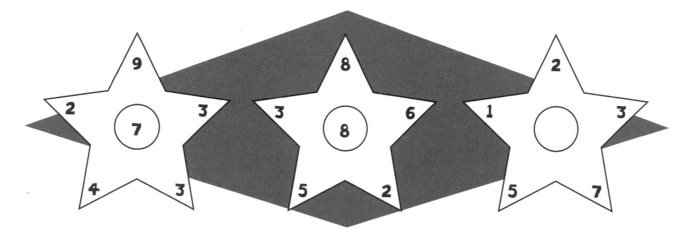

48. Trio

Using the first two circles as an example, fill in the empty segment.

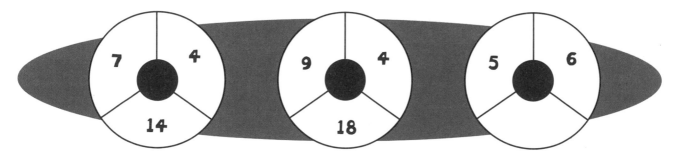

49. Grid Lock

Can you work out which numbers are required to complete grids A&B?

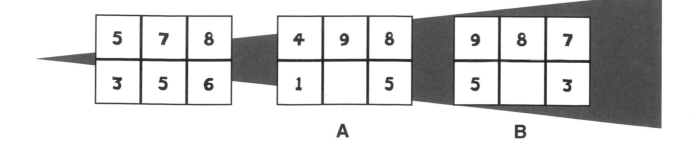

50. Vowel Play

All the vowels have been taken out of this crossword and placed in boxes next to the grid. Can you replace them all in their correct positions?

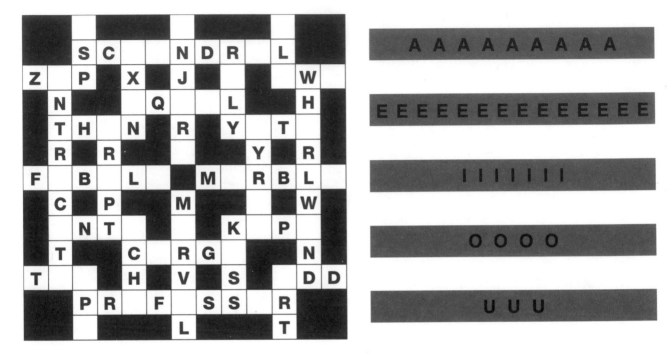

A A A A A A A A A

E E E E E E E E E E E E E E

I I I I I I I

O O O O

U U U

51. Anagram Timer

The answer to each of the clues is an anagram of the word above and below it, plus or minus one letter.

1 - Watch band

2 - Famous person

3 - Sewer rodent

4 - Plan to catch someone / something

5 - Social gathering

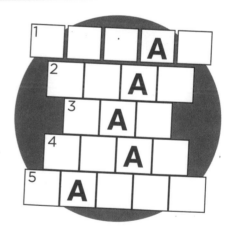

52. Odd One Out

Which number is the odd one out in each oval?

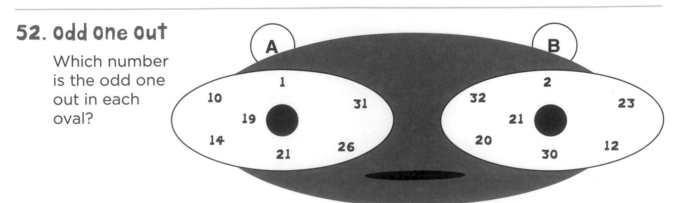

53. Proverbs

Here are three very famous proverbs with some missing words. From the choices we have given you can you complete them all?

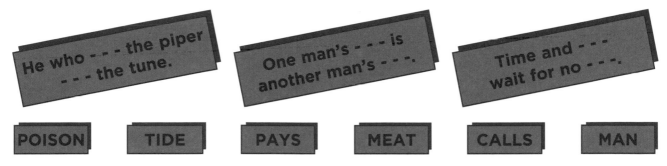

He who - - - the piper - - - the tune.

One man's - - - is another man's - - -.

Time and - - - wait for no - - -.

POISON   TIDE   PAYS   MEAT   CALLS   MAN

54. Opposites Attract

Match the four words on the left with a word of opposite meaning on the right.

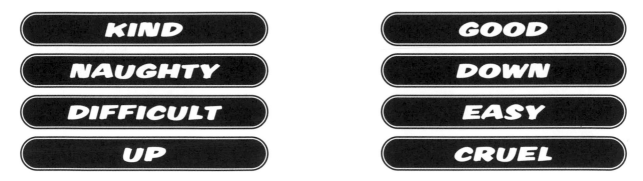

KIND   GOOD
NAUGHTY   DOWN
DIFFICULT   EASY
UP   CRUEL

55. Mix-Up

Unravel the letters to find four countries.

ECFNRA   DLOHLNA

RAKDNEM   GRALTPOU

56. Add-A-Letter

Add the same letter to all these words to make a brand new one.
e.g. The letter 't' can be added to moral to make mortal.

BID   HEAD
COCK   TIED
BEAST   STAND
CANE   TIP

57. Boxing Clever

Which number completes this sequence?

4   5   7   11   ?

58. Missing Numbers

Which numbers are missing from the empty grid?
(Clue: Look at the matching segments – the middle circle is the link!)

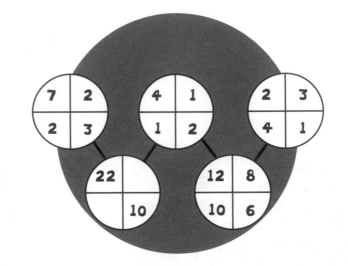

59. Honeycomb

Which number is the odd one out?

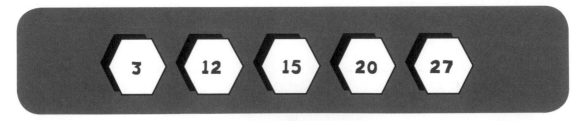

3   12   15   20   27

60. Hole Numbers

Complete this puzzle by adding the correct number to the empty circle.
(Clue: Straight thinking will not help you with this one!)

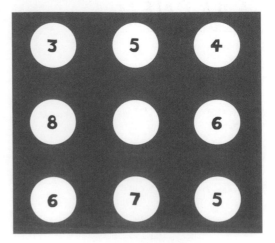

61. crossword

A regular crossword for you to enjoy. Try working it out by using the clues, but if you get stuck, the answers appear on the bottom of the page in alphabetical order.

Across

1 - Clever, capable (4)
5 - Evening dress (4)
8 - Hair clip (5)
10 - Baby's toy (6)
11 - Shine (6)
12 - Small poisonous snake (5)
14 - Line where two pieces of material are sewn together (4)
16 - Milky-white gemstone (4)
19 - Measure of land (4)
20 - *Home and - - -*, TV soap (4)
21 - Aid for measuring distances (7)
22 - Plus, as well as (4)
24 - Article on a list (4)
26 - Facial feature (4)
28 - Fly upwards (4)
30 - Association for eggheads! (5)
34 - Doing something (6)
35 - Very happy (6)
36 - A very big person (5)
37 - Pastry with jam or fruit on it (4)
38 - Area, region (4)

Down

1 - Ghostly quality (4)
2 - Part of the alphabet (6)
3 - Toboggan (4)
4 - Lazy (4)
6 - Robin Hood, for example (6)
7 - Oasis singer, - - - Gallagher (4)
8 - Put down noisily (4)
9 - Europe's single currency (4)
13 - Cleaning aid (7)
14 - Small oar (5)
15 - Greek fable writer (5)
17 - Area covered with paving stones (5)
18 - Not now! (5)
23 - Female relative (6)
25 - Drawing on the skin (6)
27 - Fog and smoke mixture (4)
28 - Condiment put on food to give it flavour (4)
29 - Something known to be true (4)
31 - *Noddy* author, - - - Blyton (4)
32 - Despatched (4)
33 - Brim, border (4)

ABLE
ACRE
ACTION
ADDER
AESOP
ALSO
AURA
AWAY
DUSTPAN
EDGE
ELATED
ENID
EURO
FACT

GIANT
GOWN
IDLE
ITEM
LATER
LETTER
LIPS
LUSTRE
MENSA
NOEL
OPAL
OUTLAW
PATIO
RATTLE

SALT
SCULL
SEAM
SENT
SEXTANT
SISTER
SLAM
SLED
SLIDE
SMOG
SOAR
TART
TATTOO
ZONE

62. Scrambled!

The answers to these clues have all been scrambled up.
Can you work out what each answer is?

1	NTERUVADE	Exciting experience
2	IARDRERSSEH	Barber
3	ARBELEISM	Very unhappy
4	GIARFEL	Delicate
5	PSANOHTS	Photograph
6	MADNARG	Parent's mother
7	AHEVBE	Be good!
8	TBLALEN	Team game
9	RMAEPTNIS	Chewing gum flavour
10	NCYFA ERSDS	Party costume (5,5)
11	UAEBSEC	For that reason
12	NIELKWR	Skin crease

63. Figure-It-Out

Which four-figure answer is missing from the empty box?

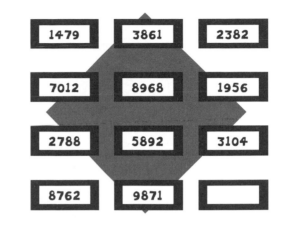

1479	3861	2382
7012	8968	1956
2788	5892	3104
8762	9871	

64. Shape Up

Find the missing number to complete the puzzle.

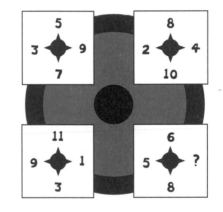

65. Take Away

What number goes in the middle oval? (Clue: It has got nothing to do with sums!)

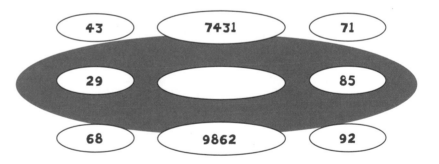

43	7431	71
29		85
68	9862	92

66. Dotty!

Which of the bottom numbers will go into the centre dot?

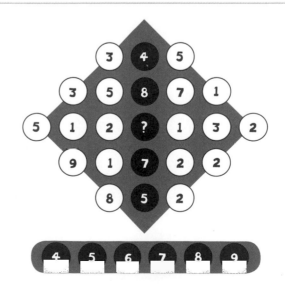

4 5 6 7 8 9

67. Twins

Pair up each word in the first circle with a word of similar meaning in the second. When you have finished, one word from each circle will be left without a twin.

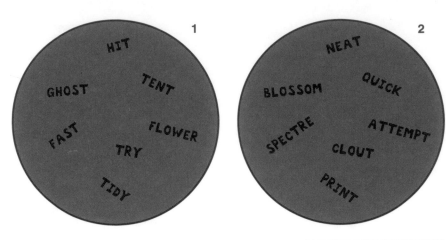

68. Star Struck

Using the first two stars as an example, find the missing number.

69. Trio

Using the first two circles as an example, fill in the empty segment.

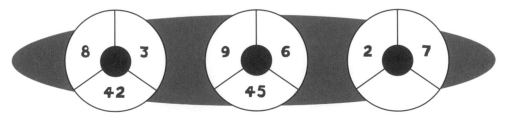

70. Grid Lock

Can you work out which numbers are required to complete grids A&B?

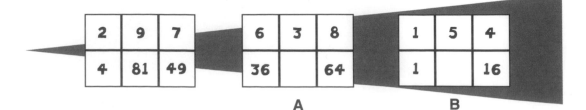

71. All change

Rearrange the words in each row to make a new one. Write it in the same line in the second box. Sometimes you will be able to make more than one word, so we have given a clue to help you. Another five-letter word will appear in the shaded column.

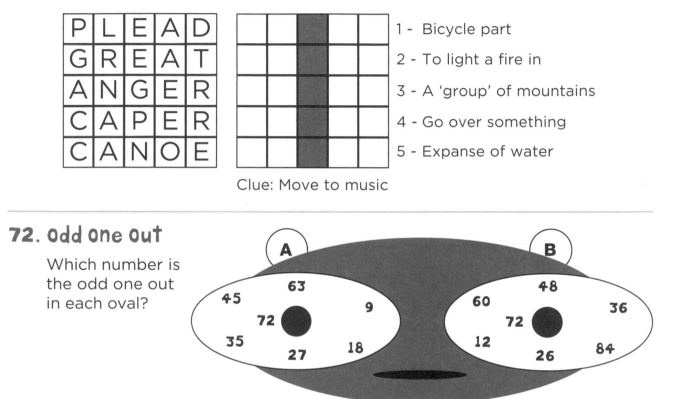

P	L	E	A	D
G	R	E	A	T
A	N	G	E	R
C	A	P	E	R
C	A	N	O	E

1 - Bicycle part

2 - To light a fire in

3 - A 'group' of mountains

4 - Go over something

5 - Expanse of water

Clue: Move to music

72. Odd One Out

Which number is the odd one out in each oval?

A: 45, 63, 72, 9, 35, 27, 18

B: 60, 48, 72, 36, 12, 26, 84

73. Watch Out

Look carefully at the sequence of watches and fill in the blank.

11:53   02:35   05:23   04:42   [blank]

A 14:23   B 02:50   C 11:34   D 07:22

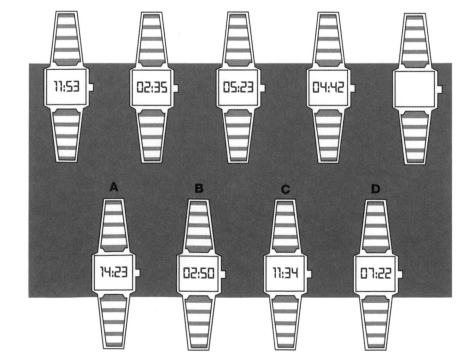

74. crossword

A regular crossword for you to enjoy. Try working it out by using the clues, but if you get stuck, the answers appear on the bottom of the page in alphabetical order.

Across

- 1 - Song from an opera (4)
- 5 - Every (4)
- 8 - Higher than (5)
- 10 - Promise, guarantee (6)
- 11 - Person in charge of a newspaper (6)
- 12 - Without anybody else (5)
- 14 - Animal with a shell, claws and ten legs (4)
- 16 - Clean and tidy (4)
- 19 - Bring up (4)
- 20 - Fleshy-leaved herb, - - - Vera (4)
- 21 - Stud or sleeper, for example (7)
- 22 - A pile of things (4)
- 24 - Vegetable that tastes like an onion (4)
- 26 - Old stringed instrument (4)
- 28 - Hand over for a price (4)
- 30 - Break or destroy something (5)
- 34 - Artificial hairpiece (6)
- 35 - Tiny wave on the surface of water (6)
- 36 - Very quick (5)
- 37 - High-pitched sound (4)
- 38 - Money that you owe someone (4)

Down

- 1 - Slightly open (4)
- 2 - Take out a policy (6)
- 3 - Adam and Eve's second son (4)
- 4 - Place where food can be baked or roasted (4)
- 6 - Real (6)
- 7 - Cause injury (4)
- 8 - Person living in Arabia? (4)
- 9 - Biblical garden (4)
- 13 - To shock greatly (7)
- 14 - Very unkind (5)
- 15 - Skilled, proficient (5)
- 17 - Large bird that hunts and eats small animals (5)
- 18 - Cloth used for drying things that are wet (5)
- 23 - Season between summer and winter (6)
- 25 - Pass by, like time (6)
- 27 - Large water jug (4)
- 28 - Slide out of control (4)
- 29 - Foot movement (4)
- 31 - Back part of an object (4)
- 32 - A baby's cot (4)
- 33 - Opening for fumes to escape through (4)

ABEL	CRUEL	NEAT
ABOVE	DEBT	OUTRAGE
ACTUAL	EACH	OVEN
ADEPT	EAGLE	PING
AJAR	EARRING	RAPID
ALOE	EDEN	REAR
ALONE	EDITOR	RIPPLE
ARAB	ELAPSE	SELL
ARIA	EWER	SKID
ASSURE	HARM	STEP
AUTUMN	HEAP	TOUPEE
BRED	INSURE	TOWEL
CRAB	LEEK	VENT
CRIB	LUTE	WRECK

75. Star Struck

Using the first two stars as an example, find the missing number.

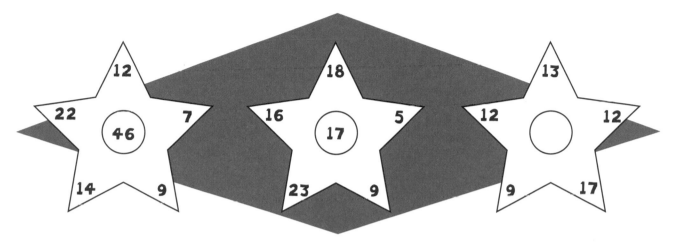

76. Trio

Using the first two circles as an example, fill in the empty segment.

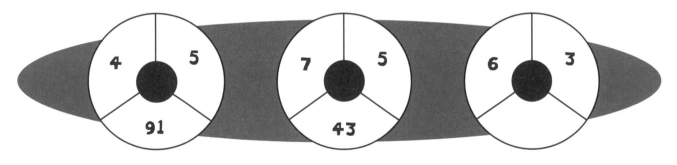

77. Grid Lock

Can you work out which numbers are required to complete grids A&B?

23	38	16
48	22	16
17	15	14

37	24	16
18	53	17
19		15

A

16	23	12
37	42	16
17		10

B

78. Wheel Spin

Which letter replaces the question mark and completes the word?

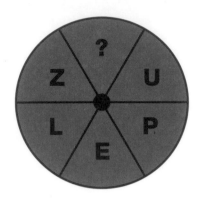

79. Next-In-Line

Which of the words below will logically follow on from these?

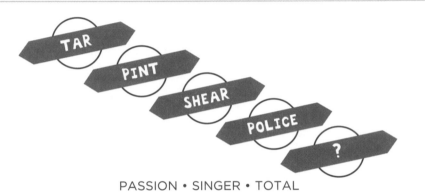

PASSION • SINGER • TOTAL

80. Dominoes

By counting the dots on these dominoes, can you work out which of the six spare pieces completes the sequence?

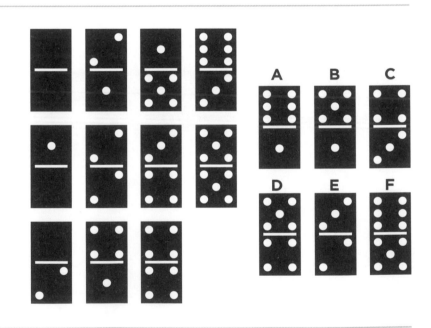

81. Cross Over

Which number is missing from each puzzle?

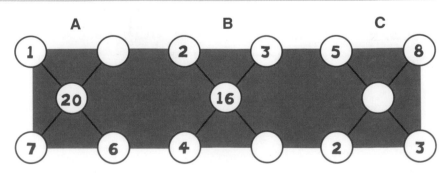

ANSWERS

1. Odd One Out:
Oval A = 2 It is the only even number.
Oval B = 15 It is the only odd number.

2. Watch Out: Answer = C The time increases by 1 hour and 5 minutes each step.

3. Pyramid Poser: Answer = 12 Add the bottom two numbers together to get the top number. 3 + 7 = 10; 6 + 3 = 9; 8 + 4 = 12

4. All Square: Add the three outer numbers and write the answer in the inner corner.

5. Add-A-Letter: Add the letter T to make the following words.
STILL STAND TRIM PLEAT
THORN TOOT FLUTE TRUE

6. Hidden Words: You can find the following gemstones hidden amongst the sentences. 1. Ruby; 2. Diamond; 3. Opal; 4. Topaz; 5. Pearl

7. Odd One Out: MELBOURNE. Because the rest are European.

8. First and Last:
TALK SEVEN MINI SCARF TILE
KILL NEW ICE FUEL EGO
New word = KNIFE

9. Dominoes: Answer = D The dots on the dominoes in the last column equal the total of all the other dots in the same row.

10. Cross Over: The middle number in each case is made up of the outer numbers, so that: A = 2 4 + 7 + 1 + 2 = 14
B = 2 5 + 1 + 3 + 2 = 11; C = 6 1 + 8 + 2 + 6 = 17

11. Tri-Pie: Answer = 18 Moving clockwise around each circle, starting with the lowest number, the numbers increase by 1, then 2, then 3 etc.

12. Number Box: Answer = 1 Add together the first and second numbers in each line to get the third. 3 + 4 = 7; 2 + 1 = 3; 5 + 5 = 10

13. All Star: Answer = 5 In each star the top number will divide into the other numbers.

14. Circles: Answer = 9 Add together the numbers on the end of each line to get the middle number.

15. Boxing Clever: Answer = 17 Double each number and subtract 1 to get the next.

16. Crossword:

F	I	S	H		A		E		T	E	A	K
E		T		E	R	O	D	E		X		N
E	U	R	O	P	E		I	C	I	C	L	E
D		E		E	A	R	T	H		U		W
	C	A	S	E		A		O	A	S	T	
R	A	M	P			G			D	E	R	V
	B		A	U	S	T	R	I	A			U
B	E	S	T		I			P	E	C	K	
		R	E	E	F		M	S	T	Y	E	
D		T		O	P	E	R	A		E		F
R	E	T	I	R	E		A	N	T	L	E	R
U		E		M	A	N	S	E		E		E
M	O	R	E		T		P		S	T	U	D

17. Five Star: 1. A (PANSY) 2. D (DAISY) 3. P (POPPY)

18. Rogue Word: CHARMER The other words all mean the same thing

19. Anagram Timer: 1. CHARM; 2. HARM; 3. ARM; 4. MARE; 5. DREAM

20. Missing Numbers: Answer = 9 and 9
The numbers in each of the segments in the bottom circles are equal to the sum of the corresponding segments in the connected circles above. Left and centre circles:
2 + 7 = 9 4 + 1 = 5 3 + 2 = 5 1 + 5 = 6
Centre and right circles:
7 + 2 = 9 1 + 3 = 4 2 + 4 = 6 5 + 4 = 9

21. Honeycomb: Answer = 22
All the other numbers are odd.

22. Hole Numbers: Answer = 37
Starting in the top left corner and moving clockwise in a spiral pattern towards the centre, add 1, then 2, then 3 etc.

23. Proverbs: A MISS is as good as a MILE
Every DOG is allowed one BITE
Great OAKS from little acorns GROW

24. Opposites Attract:
OUT DARK SWEET FAST
IN LIGHT SOUR SLOW

25. Mix-Up: 1. CARROT; 2. CABBAGE; 3. SWEDE; 4. PARSNIP

26. Tri-Pie: Answer = 7 Add together the matching segments from the two circles on the right and transfer the answer to the corresponding segment in the third circle.

27. Number Box: Answer = 6 Multiply together the first and second numbers in each line to get the third.
2 x 3 = 6; 3 x 1 = 3; 6 x 3 = 18

28. Add-A-Letter: Add the letter N to make the following words.
CANTER PANT NICE DUNE
SLANT SPLINT PINE BENT

29. Hidden Words: You can find the following birds hidden amongst the sentences.
1. Puffin; 2. Eagle; 3. Hawk; 4. Kite; 5. Sparrow

30. Figure It Out: Answer = 989
Add the two outer numbers to get the middle number.

31. Shape Up: Answer = 2
Add together each pair of opposite numbers to get the same total.

32. CROSSWORD:

F	I	L	E		A		E		B	O	S	S
L		A		I	M	P	L	Y		X		E
A	T	T	I	R	E		S	E	E	T	H	E
N		T		A	N	G	E	L		A		M
	S	E	A	N		R		P	A	I	R	
E	A	R	L		A		B	L	O	T		
	R		T	O	R	N	A	D	O		M	
V	A	S	E		I		D	R	A	B		
	H	E	R	O		T		D	E	A	N	
P		C		W	H	E	R	E		V		L
A	N	T	H	E	A		A	N	G	I	N	A
C		O		N	I	F	T	Y		N		N
T	U	R	N		R		E		W	E	R	E

33. Wheel Spin: The letter O replaces the question mark to make the word SCHOOL.

34. Take Away: Answer = 3734
Put the two digits from the right hand side in the middle of the two digits from the left hand side.

35. Dotty: Answer = 6
Add together the numbers on the left - hand side of the shaded column, then add together the numbers on the right and the difference is shown in the centre.

36. Vowel Play:

37. Next-In-Line: The word UNION follows on as the words start with vowels, A, E, I, O, U

38. Line Up: Line B = 13; Line C = 5; Line D = 6; Line E = 9; Line F = 8 Moving along the rows, add three and then subtract 1 and continue this sequence until the end.

39. Change It: Answer = 18 The number in the centre is mid-way between the outer two numbers in each segment.

40. Codebreaker:

41. Scrambled: 1. PORRIDGE; 2. SHOULDER; 3. CAPITAL; 4. HISTORY; 5. FUNFAIR; 6. MAGICIAN; 7. POCKET MONEY; 8. UNHAPPY; 9. TOURIST; 10. NEIGHBOUR; 11. CANTEEN; 12. STATION

42. Options: Answer = 15 Moving down the first column, up the second and down the third, add three each step.

ANSWERS

43. Five Star: 1. G (EAGLE); 2. G (GOOSE); 3. N (FINCH)

44. Rogue Word: WASTE The other words all mean the same thing

45. Rogue Numbers:
A = 14   All the rest are multiples of 3
B = 14   All the rest are multiples of 4
C = 16   All the rest are multiples of 6
D = 22   All the rest are multiples of 7

46. Missing Link: Answer = 59 Moving from left to right, add an extra 2 each step.

47. Star Struck: Answer = 6
Add up the outer numbers and divide it by 3 to get the middle numbers.

48. Trio: Answer = 15
Multiply the top two numbers and divide it by two to get the bottom number.

49. Grid Lock: Answer: A = 6 and B = 4
Taking each box individually, the bottom number is three less than the top in grid A and four less in grid B.

50. Vowel Play:

51. Anagram Timer: 1. STRAP; 2. STAR; 3. RAT; 4. TRAP; 5. PARTY

52. Odd One Out: Oval A = 26 It is the only number not containing a 1. Oval B = 30 It is the only number not containing a 2.

53. Proverbs: He who PAYS the piper CALLS the tune
One mans POISON is another man's MEAT
Time and TIDE wait for no MAN

54. Opposites Attract:
KIND   CRUEL
NAUGHTY   GOOD
DIFFICULT   EASY
UP   DOWN

55. Mix-Up: 1. FRANCE; 2. DENMARK; 3. HOLLAND; 4. PORTUGAL

56. Add-A-Letter: Add the letter R to make the following words:
BIRD   CROCK   BREAST   CRANE
HEARD   TRIED   STRAND   TRIP

57. Boxing Clever: Answer = 19
Multiply each number by 2 and then subtract 3 to get the next number.

58. Missing Numbers: Answer = 6 and 6
The numbers in each of the segments in the bottom circles are equal to double the numbers in the matching segments of the connected circles above.

Left and centre circles: 7 + 4 = 11 (22); 2 + 1 = 3 (6); 2 + 1 = 3 (6); 3 + 2 = 5 (10)
Centre and right circles: 4 + 2 = 6 (12); 3 + 1 = 4 (8); 1 + 4 = 5 (10); 2 + 1 = 3 (6)

59. Honeycomb: Answer = 20 All the other numbers are multiples of three.

60. Hole Numbers: Answer = 7
Starting in the top left corner and moving clockwise in a spiral pattern towards the centre, add 2 for the next number, subtract 1 for the next, add 2, subtract 1 etc.

61. Crossword:

62. Scrambled:
1. ADVENTURE
2. HAIRDRESSER
3. MISERABLE
4. FRAGILE
5. SNAPSHOT
6. GRANDMA
7. BEHAVE
8. NETBALL
9. SPEARMINT
10. FANCY DRESS
11. BECAUSE
12. WRINKLE

63. Figure It Out: Answer = 1109 Add together the numbers in the first and third columns to get the number in the middle.

64. Shape Up: Answer = 5 The sum of the numbers in each square is 24.

65. Take Away: Answer = 9852
Take all four digits shown in each line and write them in reverse numerical order in the middle.

66. Dotty: Answer = 7 Add together the numbers in each row and divide it by 2 to get the middle number.

67. Twins: Words left out are TENT and PRINT

1	2
HIT	CLOUT
GHOST	SPECTRE
FAST	QUICK
TIDY	NEAT
TRY	ATTEMPT
FLOWER	BLOSSOM

68. Star Struck: Answer = 10 Add up the outer numbers, divide by 2 and then add 3 to get the middle numbers.

69. Trio: Answer = 41
Multiply the top two numbers and write the answer in reverse at the bottom.

70. Grid Lock: Answer: A = 9 and B = 25
Square the top numbers in each box to get the bottom number. (3x3 = 9, 5x5 = 25)

71. All change:

72. Odd One Out: Oval A = 35
It is the only number not divisible by 9.
Oval B = 26
It is the only number not divisible by 12.

73. Watch Out: Answer = A
The digits shown on each watch add up to 10 every time.

74. Crossword:

75. Star Struck: Answer = 36
Add up the outer numbers and write the answer in reverse in the middle.

76. Trio: Answer = 71
Multiply the top two numbers, subtract 1 and write the answer in reverse in the bottom segment.

77. Grid Lock: Answer: A = 14 and B = 11
The numbers in the third boxes in each row and column are the sum of the digits in the first two boxes.

78. Wheel Spin: The letter Z replaces the question mark to make the word PUZZLE.

79. Next-In-Line: The word PASSION follows on as the words increase by one letter each time, 3, 4, 5, 6 and 7

80. Dominoes: Answer = F
Moving along the lines, the dots on each domino increase by three each step.

-	2	1	6
-	1	5	3

1	2	3	5
-	2	4	5

-	4	4	6
2	1	4	5

81. Cross Over: Multiply the numbers on each end of the diagonal lines and add each answer together to get the middle number. A = 2, B = 2, C = 31